FOR LOVE OF LAURA

# FOR
# LOVE
## OF
# LAURA:
## *Poetry of Petrarch*

## A TRANSLATION BY
## MARION SHORE

*The University of Arkansas Press*

*Fayetteville 1987*

Copyright © 1987 by Marion Shore
All rights reserved
Manufactured in the United States of America
Designer: Chiquita Babb
Typeface: Linotron 202 Baskerville
Typesetter: G&S Typesetters, Inc.
Printer: Thomson-Shore, Inc.
Binder: John H. Dekker & Sons, Inc.

The paper used in this publication meets the minimum requirements of the American National Standard for Permanence of Paper for Printed Library Materials Z39.48–1984. ⊗

CXXI ("Or vedi, Amor, che giovanetta donna") first appeared in *Poems from Italy,* edited by William Jay Smith and Dana Gioia (New Rivers Press, 1985).

LIBRARY OF CONGRESS CATALOGING-IN-PUBLICATION DATA
Petrarca, Francesco, 1304–1374.
    For love of Laura.
    Italian and English.
    Includes index.
    1. Petrarca, Francesco, 1304–1374—Translations,
English.  I. Shore, Marion, 1952–  .  II. Title.
PQ4496.E23S56  1987       851'.1       85–28930
ISBN 0–938626–60–4
ISBN 0–938626–61–2 (pbk.)

*for T.B.*

*. . . Oimè, il giogo, e le catene, e i ceppi*
*eran più dolci che l'andare sciolto.*

# *Contents*

# Introduction

Francesco Petrarca (1304–1374), in his time a noted author, poet, and classical scholar, is recognized for his great influence on the emerging humanism of the Renaissance. But he is best remembered for the body of Italian poetry (relatively small compared to his Latin works) in which he immortalized his love for Laura. This poetry was a vast source of inspiration to the Renaissance, and its legacy is apparent in the growth of the sonnet cycle, the sonnet form itself, and in the set of conventions we call "Petrarchan." But there is more to Petrarch than convention. His immeasurable impact over the centuries is best explained by the originality and depth and timelessness of his lyrics.

Petrarch's poetry, which he called "Rerum vulgarium fragmenta," is today designated as his *Canzoniere*, or, as he refers to it in Sonnet I, the *Rime sparse* (scattered verse). It is "scattered" in a temporal sense, having been written over the course of a lifetime. Nevertheless, one of the most striking features of the *Rime sparse* is its strong sense of underlying unity. We do know, in fact, that Petrarch frequently revised and reordered the poems, so that they come to us as he arranged them at the end of his life. The feeling of continuity and progression among the individual lyrics is therefore no accident.

The central theme of the *Rime sparse* is, of course, Petrarch's unrequited passion for Laura. There has been

1

much discussion about her identity, but the only facts we have are those Petrarch gives us: he first saw her in the church of Saint Clare, in Avignon, on April 6, 1327, and on the same day in 1348, she died. Yet a knowledge of Laura's identity is hardly necessary for an appreciation of the poetry, from which she emerges as an idealized and highly subjective image. The tone of the *Rime sparse* is one of extreme subjectivity, and its focus is clearly not on Laura as much as on Petrarch. At its core are the descriptions of love and its varying effects on his psychological state, and it is within these very inconsistencies—the continual leaps from misery to elation, from hope to despair—that the overall unity of the *Rime sparse* makes itself felt. The stark contrasts and constant emotional shifts serve to underscore an idea even more central to the poetry than love itself—the theme of struggle. Appropriate to this theme is Petrarch's personification of love as the fierce archer god of antiquity, who, occasionally, is seen taking the poet's side and attempting to vanquish the invulnerable Laura (see XLIV, CXXI), but who more often appears as his oppressive and inescapable master and foe, who "mi punge. . . , m'abbaglia, e mi distrugge" ("pierces me, blinds me, and destroys me").

But love is not the only source of struggle for Petrarch. He portrays himself as the battlefield for various parts of his personality: his passion, his intellect, his spirituality. And underlying the joys and sorrows of love, and the ongoing struggle between spirit and flesh, is a sense of the futility of all things worldly. This theme becomes even more pronounced after Laura's death. The poet is grief-stricken at her absence and obsessed with her fleshly dissolution, with the thought that her beauty has become "poca polvere"—a bit of dust. More than ever he seeks spiritual solace, which he sometimes finds in the image of the heavenly Laura who, at last, seems to pity his suffering. But such glimpses are fleeting, and provide little comfort for his abiding sense of loss. Petrarch's most vivid vision of Laura occurs in the beautiful "Levommi il mio penser in parte ov'era" (CCCII), in which she takes his hand, and reassures him that he will join her in heaven. Perhaps the shattering of a dream has never been so poignantly expressed as in the single line: "Deh perché tacque? et allargò la mano?" ("Why did she fall silent, and open her hand?").

At the end of "Levommi il mio penser," Petrarch declares that at the sound of Laura's words he nearly stayed in heaven. There is a recurring death wish in the *Rime sparse* which becomes more intense after Laura's death. In the strangely ambivalent "Non pò far Morte il dolce viso amaro" (CCCLVIII), he describes both Laura and Christ as his guides to heaven, but in the conclusion it becomes clear that he yearns not for his soul's salvation, but to escape his grief and to rejoin his lady.

In the end, it is not Laura who is to guide the poet to heaven. His love for her, even after her death, is an earthly passion and a source of struggle. In the first sonnet, Petrarch's apology to the reader, he describes the things of the world as "breve sogno"—a fleeting dream. The last sonnet (CCCLXV) is almost a reprise of the first, except that here he seeks pardon not of his fellow man, but of God. He repents of having pursued a "breve sogno," and places himself in the hands of his Creator, who, he concludes, is the only source of fulfillment and peace. Yet even this resolution is expressed not as a triumph over his struggling spirit, but as only a hope. He is still painfully aware of his mortal frailty and his likelihood to stray.

In Sonnet I, Petrarch expresses the hope that where there are those who have experienced love, he will find compassion. This is no vain appeal, for surely Petrarch speaks to everyone who "per prova intenda amore." But perhaps an even stronger appeal to our sympathy lies in his evocation of the complexity of the human spirit. With clarity and insight, he depicts a conflict that is both intimate and universal—the struggle of the different parts of a man's being. It is a struggle that is never resolved, and that ultimately takes its toll. At the end of the *Rime sparse* there is the poignant sense that when Petrarch turns at last to God, it is not in piety and resignation, but in weariness and despair.

# *Translator's Note*

The 366 poems of Petrarch's *Rime sparse* divide into two parts, generally designated as "In vita e in morte di Madonna Laura." In my translation I have attempted to capture something of the spirit of both sections, as well as a sense of the continuity of the entire work. On such a limited scale it is hardly possible to convey the full range of Petrarch's moods, nuances and ideas. Nor are all of his poetic forms represented: I have included only sonnets and madrigals, and none of the numerous *ballate, canzoni* and *sestine* of the original. Nevertheless, I have endeavored to present at least some idea of Petrarch's thematic unity, as well as a sampling of his most exceptional gems. As such, I think the poems speak for themselves, but I have provided notes for points that might require explanation.

Rather than translating Petrarch into language that is strictly modern or colloquial, I felt it more appropriate to employ a diction and vocabulary somewhat evocative of English Renaissance poetry. I have aspired to be faithful not only to the poet's tone, but to his forms, and with the exception of one sonnet,* I have duplicated the original rhyme patterns. I have used full or nearly full rhymes, as anything less would destroy the

---

*Try as I might, I was unable to render Sonnet CCCXI ("Quel rosigniuol, che sì soave piagne") into the original pattern (ABABABA-BCDCCDC), and finally settled on my own (ABBAABBACDECDE).

tight structure and musicality of the poems. At the same time, I have striven to be scrupulously faithful to his *meaning*. I was often forced to sacrifice sense for sound, but I have taken care that such departures should never stray radically from the message and spirit of the original.

All too frequently the somewhat disparaging adjectives applied to the Petrarchan tradition—formal, affected, artificial—are applied to Petrarch himself. He is often guilty of the faults ascribed to Petrarchism, but at his best, he is much more. It is my aim to help dispel the prevalent myth that Petrarch is insincere, or cerebral, or rhetorical—a myth which many stilted, passionless modern translations may have done a good deal to further—and to render what I consider the true spirit of his best poetry.

Any translation is a doomed endeavor—as Henry Adams put it: "One's translation is bound to be full of gross blunders, but the supreme blunder is that of translating at all when one is trying to catch not a fact, but a feeling." Above all, I have tried to do justice to the feeling of this poetry—its intimacy, its sweetness, its deep passion. If I have had any success, I hope I may attribute it to my master Petrarch's guiding spirit. The failures are of course my own.

# The Rime Sparse

Portrait of Petrarch from the Manuscript
*De Viris Illustribus* (1379).
Bibliothèque Nationale, Paris.

*During the Life of*
*Lady Laura*

# I

Voi ch'ascoltate in rime sparse il suono
di quei sospiri ond'io nudriva 'l core
in sul mio primo giovenile errore
quand'era in parte altr'uom da quel ch'i' sono,
    del vario stile in ch'io piango e ragiono
fra le vane speranze e 'l van dolore,
ove sia chi per prova intenda amore
spero trovar pietà, non che perdono.
    Ma ben veggio or sì come al popol tutto
favola fui gran tempo, onde sovente
di me medesmo meco mi vergogno;
    e del mio vaneggiar vergogna è 'l frutto,
e 'l pentersi, e 'l conoscer chiaramente
che quanto piace al mondo è breve sogno.

*I*

You who hear within my scattered verse
the troubled sighs on which I fed my heart
in youthful error, now that I in part
am someone other than I was at first;
　for all the varied ways I cry and curse
amid the empty hope and wasted art,
I ask that those who suffer by Love's dart
may pardon me, and pity me my worst.
　But now when I reflect how I became
a common tale to all, it brings me grief,
so that I grow ashamed that now it seems
　the fruit of all my wandering is shame,
and true repentance, and the clear belief
that what the world adores are fleeting dreams.

# I I

Per fare una leggiadra sua vendetta,
e punire in un dì ben mille offese,
celatamente Amor l'arco riprese,
come uom ch'a nocer luogo e tempo aspetta.
　Era la mia virtute al cor ristretta
per far ivi e negli occhi sue difese
quando 'l colpo mortal là giù discese
ove solea spuntarsi ogni saetta;
　però turbata nel primiero assalto
non ebbe tanto né vigor né spazio
che potesse al bisogno prender l'arme,
　overo al poggio faticoso et alto
ritrarmi accortamente da lo strazio
del quale oggi vorrebbe, e non pò aitarme.

# *I I*

To take his sweet revenge on me at last
and right a thousand wrongs with one swift blow,
in secret Love took up his deadly bow
and lay in ambush for me as I passed.
　　All my old resistance was amassed
about my heart to guard against the foe,
when the mortal arrow chanced to go
where every dart was blunted in the past;
　　thus shattered in the first attack, my will
had neither time nor vigor to remain
and arm itself against the coming darts,
　　nor strength to climb the steep and lofty hill
wherein it might escape the grievous pain
from which it would, but cannot shield my heart.

# I X

Quando 'l pianeta che distingue l'ore
ad albergar col Tauro si ritorna,
cade vertù da l'infiammate corna
che veste il mondo di novel colore;
   e non pur quel che s'apre a noi di fore,
le rive e i colli di fioretti adorna,
ma dentro dove già mai non s'aggiorna
gravido fa di sé il terrestro umore,
   onde tal frutto e simile si colga:
così costei ch'è tra le donne un sole
in me movendo de' begli occhi i rai
   crïa d'amor penseri, atti, e parole;
ma come ch'ella gli governi o volga
primavera per me pur non è mai.

## I X

When the planet that denotes the hour
returns to rest in Taurus every year,
such virtue issues from the fiery sphere
that all the world below is clad in flower;
    and not in this alone we see its power,
on hills and banks where tender buds appear,
but underground where all is cold and drear,
seeds awaken in the earth's dark bower,
    wherein such fruit is born as we can see;
and so this lady, who outshines the rest,
and turns a gaze upon me like the sun,
    engenders thoughts of love within my breast;
but, however much she looks at me,
in all this time my spring has not begun.

# XII

Se la mia vita da l'aspro tormento
si può tanto schermire, e dagli affanni,
ch'i' veggia per vertù degli ultimi anni,
donna, de' be' vostr'occhi il lume spento,
    e i cape' d'oro fin farsi d'argento,
e lassar le ghirlande e i verdi panni,
e 'l viso scolorir che ne' miei danni
a llamentar mi fa pauroso e lento,
    pur mi darà tanta baldanza Amore
ch'i' vi discovrirò de' mei martiri
qua' sono stati gli anni, e i giorni e l'ore;
    e se' l tempo è contrario ai be' desiri,
non fia ch'almen non giunga al mio dolore
alcun soccorso di tardi sospiri.

# *X I I*

If my life find strength enough to fight
the grievous battle of each passing day,
that I may meet your gaze, years from today,
lady, when your eyes have lost their light,
    and when your golden curls have turned to white,
and vanished are your wreaths and green array,
and when your youthful hue has fled away,
whose beauty makes me tremble in its sight,
    perhaps then Love will overcome my fears
enough that I may let my secret rise
and tell you what I've suffered all these years;
    and if no flame be kindled in your eyes,
at least I may be granted for my tears
the comfort of a few belated sighs.

## X V I

Movesi il vecchierel canuto e bianco
del dolce loco ov'ha sua età fornita
e da la famigliuola sbigottita
che vede il caro padre venir manco;
    indi traendo poi l'antiquo fianco
per l'estreme giornate di sua vita
quanto più pò col buon voler s'aita,
rotto dagli anni, e dal camino stanco;
    e viene a Roma, seguendo 'l desio,
per mirar la sembianza di colui
ch'ancor lassù nel ciel vedere spera:
    così, lasso, talor vo cercand'io,
donna, quanto è possibile in altrui
la disiata vostra forma vera.

# X V I

The poor old man, arising grey and pale,
deserts his gentle hearth and quiet sleep,
and leaves the loving family, who weep
and tremble as they see their father fail;
  who, on his wasted limbs, infirm and frail,
through his final days begins to creep,
his only strength a steady will to keep
from falling down along the weary trail;
  and comes to Rome, following a desire
to seek the likeness which in little time
he hopes to see again on heaven's throne.
  Ah! Lady, thus sometimes I too aspire,
and seeking other gazes, try to find
the true and blessèd image of your own.

## X I X

Son animali al mondo de sì altera
vista che 'n contra 'l sol pur si difende;
altri, però che 'l gran lume gli offende,
non escon fuor se non verso la sera;
    et altri col desio folle che spera
gioir forse nel foco, perché splende,
provan l'altra vertù, quella che 'ncende.
Lasso, el mio loco è 'n questa ultima schera;
    ch'i' non son forte ad aspettar la luce
di questa donna, e non so fare schermi
di luoghi tenebrosi, o d'ore tarde.
    Però con gli occhi lagrimosi e 'nfermi
mio destino a vederla mi conduce;
e so ben ch'i' vo dietro a quel che m'arde.

# *X I X*

There are some creatures with such flawless sight
that they can stare unblinking at the sun;
yet there are those whose lot it is to shun
the light of day and walk abroad at night.
    Still others fly about the firelight,
their wits perhaps by shining flame undone;
alas, of that third order, I am one,
who draw unto the blaze in reckless flight!
    For I who seek the sun am much too weak
to look upon the face that is my dawn,
and in the cold and dead of night I tire;
    and therefore, sick and tearful, I am drawn
toward her whose light it is my fate to seek
and so am ever drawn unto the fire.

## X X

Vergognando talor ch'ancor si taccia,
donna, per me vostra bellezza in rima,
ricorro al tempo ch'i' vi vidi prima,
tal che null'altra fia mai che mi piaccia.
   Ma trovo peso non da le mie braccia,
né ovra da polir colla mia lima;
però l'ingegno che sua forza estima
ne l'operazïon tutto s'agghiaccia.
   Più volte già per dir le labbra apersi,
poi rimase la voce in mezzo 'l petto;
ma qual sòn poria mai salir tant'alto?
   Più volte incominciai di scriver versi;
ma la penna e la mano e l'intelletto
rimaser vinti nel primier assalto.

# X X

Ashamed sometimes, my lady, that I still
cannot express your beauty in my rhyme,
I wander to that sweet and distant time
when you alone gained power of my will.
   But even there I find no guiding skill,
no strength to scale a height I cannot climb,
for such a task demands a force sublime,
at whose attempt I fall back, mute and still.
   How often do I move my lips to speak,
and find my voice lies buried in my breast—
but then, what sound could ever rise so high?
   How often in my verses do I seek
to find the words my tongue cannot express,
but pen and hand are vanquished with each try.

# X X I

Milla fïate, o dolce mia guerrera,
per aver co' begli occhi vostri pace
v'aggio proferto il cor; ma voi non piace
mirar sì basso colla mente altera.
   E se di lui fors'altra donna spera,
vive in speranza debile e fallace:
mio, perché sdegno ciò ch'a voi dispiace,
esser non può già mai così com'era.
   Or s'io lo scaccio, et e' non trova in voi
ne l'esilio infelice alcun soccorso,
né sa star sol, né gire ov'altri il chiama,
   poria smarrire il suo natural corso;
che grave colpa fia d'ambeduo noi,
e tanto più de voi, quanto più v'ama.

# *X X I*

My warrior, a thousand times have I
surrendered you my heart that I might gain
the peace of your fair glance, you who disdain
to lower even once those lofty eyes.
    And now if any other lady try
to win its favor, she will try in vain:
for in my breast it can no more remain
since I despise the thing that you deny.
    Now if I cast it out, and if it finds
no refuge from its banishment in yours,
nor solace in another's, I am sure
    alone, it would depart from nature's course—
and then, how grave the fault, both yours and mine,
but more so yours, because it loves you more.

# X X X V

Solo e pensoso i più deserti campi
vo mesurando a passi tardi e lenti,
e gli occhi porto per fuggire intenti,
ove vestigio uman l'arena stampi.
   Altro schermo non trovo che mi scampi
dal manifesto accorger de le genti,
perché negli atti d'alegrezza spenti
di fuor si legge com'io dentro avampi:
   sì ch'io mi credo omai che monti e piagge,
e fiumi e selve sappian di che tempre
sia la mia vita, ch'è celata altrui.
   Ma pur sì aspre vie, né sì selvagge
cercar non so ch'Amor non venga sempre
ragionando con meco, et io co llui.

# *X X X V*

Alone and thoughtful, through deserted fields
I go with lowered head and measured pace,
my eyes intent that I might flee in haste
should any human footprint be revealed.
   I find no other shelter to conceal
my burning heart than some secluded place,
for once among the crowd my wretched face
betrays the very flames it hoped to shield;
   so that by now I think the hills and stones,
the rivers and the forests are aware
of the life I lead, to others dim;
   and yet I find no path so overgrown
that Love does not come with me everywhere,
speaking with me the while, and I with him.

# X X X V I

S'io credesse per morte essere scarco
del pensiero amoroso che m'atterra,
colle mie mani avrei già posto in terra
queste membra noiose, e quello incarco;
    ma perch'io temo che sarebbe un varco
di pianto in pianto, e d'una in altra guerra,
di qua dal passo ancor che mi si serra
mezzo rimango, lasso, e mezzo il varco.
    Tempo ben fora omai d'avere spinto
l'ultimo stral la dispietata corda
ne l'altrui sangue già bagnato e tinto:
    et io ne prego Amore, e quella sorda
che mi lassò de' suoi color depinto,
e di chiararmi a sé non le ricorda.

# X X X V I

 

If I believed by dying I could part
the sorrows and the yearning I endure,
then I would surely linger on no more
but by my own hand, still my weary heart;
    yet since I fear it would be but the start
of greater woe, and yet another war,
to pass from here to that forbidden shore,
alas, I half remain and half depart.
    High time it were that Love's relentless bow
which speeds so many hearts their mortal shot
had given mine by now the final blow;
    and Death, although I call him, heeds me not,
who painted me his colors long ago,
and should have come to claim me, but forgot.

# X L I V

Que' che 'n Tesaglia ebbe le man sì pronte
a farla del civil sangue vermiglia
pianse morto il marito di sua figlia,
raffigurato a le fatezze conte;
   e 'l pastor ch'a Golia ruppe la fronte
pianse la ribellante sua famiglia,
e sopra 'l buon Saul cangiò le ciglia,
ond'assai può dolersi il fiero monte.
   Ma voi che mai pietà non discolora,
e ch'avete gli schermi sempre accorti
contra l'arco d'Amor che 'ndarno tira,
   mi vedete straziare a mille morti;
né lagrima, però discese ancora
da' be' vostr'occhi, ma disdegno et ira.

# X L I V

   He who did not hesitate to stain
the countryside of Thessaly bright red,
when his daughter's husband's blood was shed
then cried out loud in bitterness and pain;
   and he by whom Goliath had been slain
lamented when his rebel son lay dead,
and wept for noble Saul with lowered head,
wherein the lofty mountain might complain.
   But you who are untouched by pity's sway,
and have all your defenses quick to shun
the darts which Love in vain attempts to fire,
   you see me by a thousand deaths undone;
yet not a tear has fallen to this day
from your fair eyes, but only scorn and ire.

# XLIX

Perch'io t'abbia guardato di menzogna
a mio podere et onorato assai,
ingrata lingua, già però non m'hai
renduto onor, ma fatto ira e vergogna;
   ché quando più 'l tuo aiuto mi bisogna
per dimandar mercede, allor ti stai
sempre più fredda, e se parole fai,
son imperfette, e quasi d'uom che sogna.
   Lagrime triste, e voi tutte le notti
m'accompagnate, ov'io vorrei star solo,
poi fuggite dinanzi a la mia pace;
   e voi sì pronti a darmi angoscia e duolo,
sospiri, allor traete lenti e rotti:
sola la vista mia del cor non tace.

## X L I X

It was to do you honor that I deemed
by means of you all falsehood to forestall,
for which, ungrateful tongue, your thanks are small,
who bring me only shame for my esteem;
    since when I need you most, then most you seem
to help me least, for at her glance you fall
mute and cold, or if you speak at all,
the words are weak and flawed, as in a dream.
    And you, unceasing tears that fill my eyes
all through the night, when I would be alone,
how fast you are, before her, to depart;
    and weary sighs, to which I am so prone,
how suddenly you freeze, and will not rise:
my face alone does not betray my heart.

# *L I I*

Non al suo amante più Dïana piacque,
quando per tal ventura tutta ignuda
la vide in mezzo de le gelide acque,
    ch'a me la pastorella alpestra e cruda
posta a bagnar un leggiadretto velo,
ch'a l'aura il vago e biondo capel chiuda;
    tal che mi fece or quand'egli arde 'l cielo
tutto tremar d'un amoroso gielo.

# *L I I*

With no more pleasure did her lover sigh
when he espied Diana bathing nude
amid the icy waters, than do I,
    who pause to watch the shepherdess, fair and crude,
and as she kneels to bathe the graceful veil
that bound her hair, so shaken is my mood,
    that all the heavens burn, to no avail—
an icy tremor fills me, and I pale.

## L I V

Perch'al viso d'Amor portava insegna,
mosse una pellegrina il mio cor vano,
ch'ogni altra mi parea d'onor men degna;
    e lei seguendo su per l'erbe verdi,
udì' dir alta voce di lontano:
—Ai, quanti passi per la selva perdi!—
    Allor mi strinsi a l'ombra d'un bel faggio,
tutto pensoso, e rimirando intorno,
vidi assai periglioso il mio viaggio;
    e tornai indietro quasi a mezzo 'l giorno.

## *L I V*

Because she bore Love's colors in her face,
a passing pilgrim led my heart astray,
beside whose worth all others must seem base;
    and through the green grass, following her, beguiled,
I heard a voice ring out from far away:
"How many steps you've wasted in the wild!"
    I paused, and of my error taking heed,
I sat beneath a shady beech, where soon
I deemed my journey perilous indeed,
    and turned around when it was barely noon.

# L X I I

Padre del ciel, dopo i perduti giorni,
dopo le notti vaneggiando spese
con quel fero desio ch'al cor s'accese
mirando gli atti per mio mal sì adorni,
   piacciati omai col tuo lume ch'io torni
ad altra vita, et a più belle imprese,
sì ch'avendo le reti indarno tese,
il mio duro adversario se ne scorni.
   Or volge, Signor mio, l'undecimo anno
ch'i' fui sommesso al dispietato giogo
che sopra i più soggetti è più feroce.
   Miserere del mio non degno affanno;
reduci i pensier vaghi a miglior luogo;
ramenta lor come oggi fusti in croce.

# L X I I

Heavenly father, after the wasted days,
after the many sleepless nights I've lain
beset by Love, the cause of all my pain,
yearning for that which set my soul ablaze,

now may it please You that I learn to raise
my spirit to a loftier domain,
that with his net spread out for me in vain,
I can elude the adversary's gaze.

And now, dear Lord, it is eleven years
since I was vanquished by my captor's might,
whose willing subjects feel his cruelest sway.

Have mercy on my undeserving tears;
conduct my thoughts unto a greater height;
remind them You were on the cross today.

## L X X V

I begli occhi ond'i' fui percosso in guisa
ch' e' medesmi porian saldar la piaga,
e non già vertù d'erbe, o d'arte maga,
o di pietra dal mar nostro divisa,
    m'hanno la via sì d'altro amor precisa,
ch'un sol dolce penser l'anima appaga,
e se la lingua di seguirlo è vaga,
la scorta pò, non ella esser derisa.
    Questi son que' begli occhi che l'imprese
del mio signor vittorïose fanno
in ogni parte, e più sovra 'l mio fianco;
    questi son que' begli occhi che mi stanno
sempre nel cor colle faville accese;
perch'io di lor parlando non mi stanco.

# L X X V

The lovely eyes that dealt unto my heart
the very wound they only can make well,
not strength of healing herb or magic spell,
or amulet brought from some distant part,
    have caused me other pleasures to depart
and with one gentle thought alone to dwell,
which if my tongue has tried in vain to tell,
the fault is with its guide, and not its art.
    These are the lovely eyes within whose light
my mighty lord gained victory of me,
in every part, but mostly in my breast;
    these are the lovely eyes whose flame I see
kindled in my heart both day and night;
for, speaking of these eyes, I cannot rest.

# L X X X I X

Fuggendo la pregione ove Amor m'ebbe
molt'anni a far di me quel ch'a lui parve,
donne mie, lungo fora a ricontarve
quanto la nova libertà m'increbbe.
Diceami il cor che per sé non saprebbe
viver un giorno, e poi tra via m'apparve
quel traditore in sì mentite larve
che più saggio di me inganato avrebbe.
Onde più volte sospirando indietro
dissi:—Oimè, il giogo, e le catene, e i ceppi
eran più dolci che l'andare sciolto.—
Misero me, che tardo il mio mal seppi!
e con quanta fatica oggi mi spetro
de l'errore, ov'io stesso m'era involto!

# *L X X X I X*

From Love's prison as I broke away,
within whose grasp for years I could not rise—
at which escape you may express surprise
to hear the way my freedom caused dismay—
my heart cried out it could not live one day
alone, when on the path before my eyes,
that traitor beckoned in his fair disguise,
who would have led a wiser man astray.
Wherein I stopped and sighing for the past,
I cried, "The yoke, the shackles, and the chain
were sweeter to my heart than freedom's taste!"
Alas, too late again, I know my pain,
and with what weakness struggle now at last
to flee the error I myself embraced!

# XCIII

Più volte Amor m'avea già detto:—Scrivi,
scrivi quel che vedesti in lettre d'oro,
sì come i miei seguaci discoloro,
e 'n un momento gli fo morti e vivi.
    Un tempo fu che 'n te stesso 'l sentivi,
volgare esemplo a l'amoroso coro;
poi di man mi ti tolse altro lavoro;
ma già ti raggiuns'io mentre fuggivi.
    E se' begli occhi, ond'io me ti mostrai
e là dove era il mio dolce ridutto
quando ti ruppi al cor tanta durezza,
   mi rendon l'arco ch'ogni cosa spezza,
forse non avrai sempre il viso asciutto:
ch'i' mi pasco di lagrime, e tu 'l sai.—

# X C I I I

How often Love has come and told me, "Write;
write the things you've seen in words of gold,
the way I turn my followers pale and cold,
and kill them and restore them by my might.
    There was a time you felt me at my height:
a fine example to the lovelorn fold;
then other labors freed you from my hold;
but I rejoined you even in your flight.
    And if the lovely eyes, within whose glow
I found the strength to let the arrow fly
that pierced your heart's resistance once before,
    return to me the bow whose aim is sure,
perhaps you'll find your eyes are not so dry;
for I am fed by tears, as well you know." .

## C I I

Cesare, poi che 'l traditor d'Egitto
li fece il don de l'onorata testa,
celando l'allegrezza manifesta
pianse per gli occhi fuor sì come è scritto;
    et Anibàl, quando a l'imperio afflitto
vide farsi fortuna sì molesta,
rise fra gente lagrimosa e mesta
per isfogare il suo acerbo despitto.
    E così aven che l'animo ciascuna
sua passïon sotto 'l contrario manto
ricopre co la vista or chiara or bruna:
    però s'alcuna volta io rido o canto,
facciol perch'i' non ho se non quest'una
via da celare il mio angoscioso pianto.

## C I I

Caesar, when he saw the honored head
brought him by the false Egyptian's guile,
hid within his heart a joyful smile
and poured forth sorry tears, as it is said;
   and Hannibal, when all his luck had fled
and left his reign afflicted by such trial,
amid the weeping masses all the while,
to ease his bitter sorrow, laughed instead.
   And thus the heart attempts with false display
to hide its disposition bright or drear
beneath a cloak, now sorrowful, now gay:
   so if sometimes you see me full of cheer,
it is because I know no other way
than this, to hide my dark and bitter tears.

## C V I

Nova angeletta sovra l'ale accorta
scese dal cielo in su la fresca riva,
là 'nd'io passava sol per mio destino.
   Poi che senza compagna e senza scorta
mi vide, un laccio che di seta ordiva
tese fra l'erba, ond'è verde il camino.
   Allor fui preso, e non mi spiacque poi,
sì dolce lume uscìa degli occhi suoi.

# C V I

I saw a wondrous angel lightly glide
above the verdant bank whereon I passed,
and seeing that I walked, as was my use,
    alone with neither company nor guide,
she came and stood beside me on the grass
along the road, and stretched a silken noose.
    Thus was I taken, yet I gave no cry,
so sweetly did the light shine in her eyes.

# C X I I

Sennuccio, i' vo' che sapi in qual manera
trattato sono, e qual vita è la mia:
ardomi e struggo ancor com'io solia,
l'aura mi volve, e son pur quel ch'i' m'era.
    Qui tutta umile, e qui la vidi altera,
or aspra, or piana, or dispietata, or pia;
or vestirsi onestate, or leggiadria,
or mansueta, or disdegnosa e fera;
    qui cantò dolcemente, e qui s'assise;
qui si rivolse, e qui rattenne il passo;
qui co' begli occhi mi trafisse il core;
    qui disse una parola, e qui sorrise;
qui cangiò 'l viso. In questi pensier, lasso,
notte e dì tiemmi il signor nostro Amore.

# C X I I

Sennuccio, I would tell you how I fare,
the way I yearn and pass my life away:
for what I was, I fear I am today;
still borne upon the wind, and full of care.

Here I saw her meek, here proud and fair,
now pitiless and stern, now kind and gay,
now chastely clad, and now in fine array,
now fierce and cold, now with a gentle air.

Here she sang, and here she sat awhile,
here she paused, and here I saw her pass,
here those eyes pierced through me with their light,

here she spoke a word, and here she smiled,
here she frowned. And in such thoughts, alas,
our master Love retains me day and night.

# C X X I

Or vedi, Amor, che giovenetta donna
tuo regno sprezza, e del mio mal non cura;
e tra duo ta' nemici è sì secura.
　　Tu se' armato, et ella in treccie e 'n gonna
si siede e scalza, in mezzo i fiori e l'erba,
ver' me spietata, e 'ncontra te superba.
　　I' son pregion, ma se pietà ancor serba
l'arco tuo saldo, e qualcuna saetta,
fa di te, e di me, signor vendetta.

# C X X I

Now Love, see how this lady, young and fair,
disdains your might, and grants my ills no cure;
with two such foes, so heedless and secure.
    You travel armed, while she, with braided hair,
goes roaming barefoot through the fields in flower,
so cold to me, so scornful of your power.
    A prisoner now, I wait upon the hour
when you my lord, with one unfailing dart
avenge at last your honor and my heart.

# C X X I V

Amor, Fortuna, e la mia mente schiva
di quel che vede, e nel passato volta,
m'affliggon sì ch'io porto alcuna volta
invidia a quei che son su l'altra riva.
Amor mi strugge 'l cor, Fortuna il priva
d'ogni conforto, onde la mente stolta
s'adira e piange, e così in pena molta
sempre conven che combattendo viva.
Né spero i dolci dì tornino indietro,
ma pur di male in peggio quel ch'avanza;
e di mio corso ho già passato 'l mezzo.
Lasso, non di diamante, ma d'un vetro
veggio di man cadermi ogni speranza,
e tutt'i miei pensier romper nel mezzo.

# C X X I V

Love and Fortune and my mind, made sore
by what it sees, and dwelling in the past,
oppress me so, that I have come at last
to envy those upon the other shore.
    Love inflicts the wound whose only cure
Fortune will not grant, so that, aghast,
my mind bears arms against a pain so vast
that every day I live as if at war.
    Nor will I see the pleasures left behind,
but in the midst of greater pain shall stand,
and I am past the middle of my day.
    Alas, unlike a diamond do I find
the shining hope I held within my hand,
that now, like glass, lies shattered by the way.

# C X X X I I I

Amor m'ha posto come segno a strale,
come al sol neve, come cera al foco,
e come nebbia al vento, e son già roco,
donna, mercé chiamando, e voi non cale.
　　Dagli occhi vostri uscìo 'l colpo mortale,
contra cui non mi val tempo né loco;
da voi sola procede, e parvi un gioco,
il sole, e 'l foco, e 'l vento, ond'io son tale.
　　I pensier son saette, e 'l viso un sole,
e 'l desir foco, e 'nseme con quest'arme
mi punge Amor, m'abbaglia, e mi distrugge;
　　e l'angelico canto, e le parole,
col dolce spirto, ond'io non posso aitarme,
son l'aura inanzi a cui mia vita fugge.

# C X X X I I I

I am to Love as target to a dart,
as snow to blazing sun, as wax to flame,
as fog to wind; and yet I call your name,
my voice grown hoarse before your scornful heart.
    With your eyes you let the blow depart,
and I could find no shelter from their aim;
and in that single glance at once there came
the sun, the flame, the wind, wherein I smart.
    My thoughts are darts, the sunlight is your face,
desire is a flame, and with these arms
Love inflames my heart and blinds my eyes;
    and in that angel voice and gentle grace,
that blissful aura, cause of all my harms,
awaits the death to which my spirit flies.

# C X L V

Ponmi ove 'l sole occide i fiori e l'erba,
o dove vince lui il ghiaccio e la neve;
ponmi ov'è 'l carro suo temprato e leve,
et ov'è chi cel rende, o chi cel serba;
    ponmi in umil fortuna, od in superba,
al dolce aere sereno, al fosco e greve;
ponmi a la notte, al dì lungo ed al breve,
a la matura etate od a l'acerba;
    ponmi in cielo, od in terra, od in abisso,
in alto poggio, in valle ima e palustre,
libero spirto, od a' suoi membri affisso;
    ponmi con fama oscura, o con illustre;
sarò qual fui, vivrò com'io son visso,
continuando il mio sospir trilustre.

# C X L V

Put me where the sun burns cruel and bright,
or where cold tempests drive the light away,
put me where its beams are fair and gay,
or where it rises, or descends at night;
   put me in high rank or humble plight,
where air is sweet and calm, or bleak and grey,
put me in night, in long or fleeting day,
in age's ripeness, or in youth's delight;
   put me on earth, in heaven, or dark hell,
an errant soul, or bound by mortal frame,
upon a hill, in marshland low and fell;
   put me in fate obscure, or shining fame;
I will not change, wherever I may dwell:
my love will last, my heart will be the same.

# CLIX

In qual parte del ciel, in quale idea
era l'esempio, onde Natura tolse
quel bel viso leggiadro, in ch'ella volse
mostrar qua giù quanto lassù potea?
    Qual ninfa in fonti, in selve mai qual dea,
chiome d'oro sì fino a l'aura sciolse?
quando un cor tante in sé vertuti accolse?
benché la somma è di mia morte rea.
    Per divina bellezza indarno mira
chi gli occhi di costei già mai non vide
come soavemente ella gli gira;
    non sa come Amor sana, e come ancide,
chi non sa come dolce ella sospira,
e come dolce parla, e dolce ride.

# C L I X

In what idea, in what part of the sky
did Nature find the shape she copied there,
to form a face so radiant and fair
and show below what she could do on high?
    What river nymph has ever loosed to dry
upon the wind such shining golden hair?
When was one heart so virtuous and rare?
although it is the reason that I die.
    He who seeks a glimpse of paradise
here upon this earth must vainly seek
if he has never gazed into her eyes;
    nor knows what sweet destruction Love can wreak
unless he hears the way she sweetly sighs,
and hears her sweetly laugh, and sweetly speak.

# C L X

Amor et io sì pien di meraviglia
come chi mai cosa incredibil vide,
miriam costei quand'ella parla o ride
che sol se stessa, e nulla altra simiglia.
   Dal bel seren de le tranquille ciglia
sfavillan sì le mie due stelle fide,
ch'altro lume non è ch'infiammi e guide
chi d'amar altamente si consiglia.
   Qual miracolo è quel, quando tra l'erba
quasi un fior siede, over quand'ella preme
col suo candido seno un verde cespo!
   Qual dolcezza è ne la stagione acerba
vederla ir sola coi pensier suoi inseme,
tessendo un cerchio a l'oro terso e crespo!

# C L X

Love and I are vanquished by delight,
as one who on a miracle might gaze,
when we behold her sweet and gentle ways,
who far surpasses every mortal sight.
   Within that tranquil brow, so calm and bright,
there shine the stars that set my soul ablaze,
for not another light could guide and raise
the loving heart to such a noble height.
   It seems to me a miracle to view
how, like a flower in among the grass,
she seats herself within a meadow fair!
   What loveliness it is when spring is new,
and pensive and alone I see her pass,
weaving a garland for her golden hair!

# CLXIII

Amor che vedi ogni pensero aperto
e i duri passi onde tu sol mi scorgi,
nel fondo del mio cor gli occhi tuoi porgi,
a te palese, a tutt'altri coverto.
　　Sai quel che per seguirte ho già sofferto;
e tu pur via di poggio in poggio sorgi,
di giorno in giorno, e di me non t'accorgi
che son sì stanco, e 'l sentier m'è troppo erto.
　　Ben veggio io di lontano il dolce lume
ove per aspre vie mi sproni e giri,
ma non ho come tu da volar piume.
　　Assai contenti lasci i miei desiri,
pur che ben desiando i' mi consume,
né le dispiaccia che per lei sospiri.

# CLXIII

Love who see within this weary breast
and know the dismal passes where you lead,
now turn your gaze upon my secret need,
so clear to you, and hidden from the rest.
    You know how I have suffered in your quest,
and yet from peak to peak I see you speed;
from day to day, of me you take no heed,
nor that the path is steep and I would rest.
    How well I see the sweet light shining high
above the winding pathways where I turn,
but unlike you I have no wings to fly;
    yet I am well content if I may burn
with such a noble longing, though I die,
and not displease the one for whom I yearn.

# C L X I V

Or che 'l ciel e la terra e 'l vento tace
e le fere e gli augelli il sonno affrena,
Notte il carro stellato in giro mena
e nel suo letto il mar senz'onda giace,
   vegghio, penso, ardo, piango, e chi mi sface
sempre m'è inanzi per mia dolce pena:
guerra è 'l mio stato, d'ira e di duol piena,
e sol di lei pensando ho qualche pace.
   Così sol d'una chiara fonte viva
move 'l dolce e l'amaro, ond'io mi pasco;
una man sola mi risana e punge,
   e perché 'l mio martir non giunga a riva
mille volte il dì moro, e mille nasco:
tanto da la salute mia son lunge.

# C L X I V

Now that earth and heaven and the breeze
and all the beasts are sleeping, while the night
draws his starry chariot into flight,
and dreaming and unruffled lie the seas,
   I see, I think, I weep, I burn and freeze,
while my sweet torment looms within my sight;
as if at war, enraged and weak, I fight,
and thoughts of her provide my only peace.
   Thus from a single living fount am I
sustained at once by sweet and bitter drink,
and likewise healed and wounded by one hand,
   a thousand times each day am born and die,
and cannot come to shore, and fear I sink,
so far from my salvation do I stand.

# C L X V

Come 'l candido piè per l'erba fresca
i dolci passi onestamente move,
vertù che 'ntorno i fiori apra e rinove
de le tenere piante sue par ch'esca.
    Amor che solo i cor leggiadri invesca
né degna di provar sua forza altrove,
da' begli occhi un piacer sì caldo piove
ch'i' non curo altro ben né bramo altr'esca.
    E co l'andar e col soave sguardo
s'accordan le dolcissime parole,
e l'atto mansueto, umile e tardo.
    Di tai quattro faville, e non già sole,
nasce 'l gran foco, di ch'io vivo et ardo,
che son fatto un augel notturno al sole.

# C L X V

When through the verdant meadows here and there
she moves her tender feet so pure and white,
there issues forth such virtue from the sight
that flowers spring beneath her everywhere.
 Love who takes the noble in his snare
and to the rest disdains to show his might,
from her eyes pours forth such wondrous light,
that to survive I need no other fare.
 And with that graceful step and tender gaze
accord the lovely words I hear her say,
and likewise all her sweet and gentle ways;
 and in my breast, where all these sparks hold sway,
there burns the flame that sets my heart ablaze,
who have become a bird of night by day.

# C L X X I V

Fera stella, se 'l cielo ha forza in noi
quant'alcun crede, fu sotto ch'io nacqui,
e fera cuna, dove nato io giacqui,
e fera terra, ov'e' piè mossi poi;
   e fera donna, che con gli occhi suoi,
e con l'arco, a cui sol per segno piacqui,
fe' la piaga onde, Amor, teco non tacqui
che con quell'arme risaldar la pòi.
   Ma tu prendi a diletto i dolor miei;
ella non già, perché non son più duri,
e 'l colpo è di saetta, e non di spiedo.
   Pur mi consola, che languir per lei
meglio è che gioir d'altra, e tu mel giuri
per l'orato tuo strale, et io tel credo.

# CLXXIV

If stars control our lives, as some are sure,
then I was born beneath a curséd sky,
and in a curséd cradle did I lie,
and in a curséd land began my war;
    and curséd were those eyes so bright and pure
from which I saw the deadly arrows fly,
that to my master Love alone I cry
and pray that with your might you'll grant my cure.
    But you, it seems, delight in all my pain;
not she, she would I had still more to bear;
and that you held a spear and not a bow.
    Yet better far to suffer her disdain
than win another's heart, and this you swear
by your gold shaft, and I believe it's so.

# C L X X X I X

Passa la nave mia colma d'oblio
per aspro mare, a mezza notte il verno,
enfra Scilla e Caribdi, et al governo
siede 'l signore, anzi 'l nimico mio;
    a ciascun remo un penser pronto e rio
che la tempesta e 'l fin par ch'abbi a scherno;
la vela rompe un vento umido eterno
di sospir, di speranze, e di desio;
    pioggia di lagrimar, nebbia di sdegni
bagna e rallenta le già stanche sarte,
che son d'error con ignoranzia attorto;
    celansi i duo mei dolci usati segni;
morta fra l'onde è la ragion e l'arte;
tal ch'incomincio a desperar del porto.

# C L X X X I X

My vessel with oblivion its freight
passes through a sea of bitter fears,
while at the helm my cruel master steers
between Charybdis' tides and Scylla's strait;
    at every oar a thought, in reckless state,
who seems to scorn the tempest as it nears;
the sails are beaten by a rain of tears,
and driven onward by the wind of fate;
    a fog of doubt, a torrent of disdain
bathe the deck and loose the tired rope,
that now I fear the journey must be short;
    above, my faithful stars are veiled in rain,
below, my reason founders with my hope,
and I begin despairing of the port.

# C X C

Una candida cerva sopra l'erba
verde m'apparve, con duo corna d'oro,
fra due riviere, all'ombra d'un alloro,
levando 'l sole a la stagione acerba.

Era sua vista sì dolce superba,
ch'i' lasciai per seguirla ogni lavoro,
come l'avaro che 'n cercar tesoro
con diletto l'affanno disacerba.

"Nessun mi tocchi," al bel collo d'intorno
scritto avea di diamanti e di topazi,
"libera farmi al mio Cesare parve."

Et era 'l sol già volto al mezzo giorno,
gli occhi miei stanchi di mirar, non sazi,
quand'io caddi ne l'acqua, et ella sparve.

## C X C

Upon a river bank a pure white deer
it was my fate one morning to behold,
beneath a shady laurel, in the cold
of the unripe season of the year.
So lofty and so sweet did she appear
that quickly to pursue her I made bold,
like the miser, seeking after gold,
whose pleasure makes his hardship less severe.
"Touch me not," I saw as she ran by
about her neck, in precious diamonds spelled,
"My Caesar willed that I belong to none."
And when the sun was midway through the sky
with weary and unsated eyes I fell
into the river's depths, and she was gone.

# C C I X

I dolci colli ov'io lasciai me stesso,
partendo onde partir già mai non posso,
mi vanno innanzi, et emmi ognior a dosso
quel caro peso, ch'Amor m'ha commesso.
　Meco di me mi meraviglio spesso,
ch'i' pur vo sempre, e non son ancor mosso
dal bel giogo più volte indarno scosso,
ma com' più me n'allungo, e più m'appresso.
　E qual cervo ferito di saetta,
col ferro avelenato dentr'al fianco,
fugge, e più duolsi quanto più s'affretta,
　tal io, con quello stral dal lato manco,
che mi consuma, e parte mi diletta,
di duol mi struggo, e di fuggir mi stanco.

# C C I X

The hills in which I left myself behind,
leaving the place I never can forsake,
are with me ever, though I sleep or wake,
as is that blesséd load, by Love consigned.
    Often have I marvelled that my mind
seems more unmoved with every step I take;
and from the yoke that I have tried to shake
the more I flee, the more it seems to bind.
    And like a deer who feels the stinging bite
within her bosom of a poison dart,
and suffers all the more by taking flight,
    so I am, with this arrow in my heart,
which is both my despair and my delight,
and pains me though I linger or depart.

# C C X I I

Beato in sogno e di languir contento,
d'abbracciar l'ombre e seguir l'aura estiva,
nuoto per mar che non ha fondo o riva,
solco onde, e 'n rena fondo, e scrivo in vento,
   e 'l sol vagheggio sì ch'elli ha già spento
col suo splendor la mia vertù visiva,
et una cerva errante e fugitiva
caccio con un bue zoppo, e 'nfermo, e lento.
   Cieco e stanco ad ogni altro ch'al mio danno
il qual dì e notte palpitando cerco,
sol Amor e madonna, e Morte chiamo;
   così venti anni, grave e lungo affanno,
pur lagrime e sospiri e dolor merco:
in tale stella presi l'esca e l'amo!

# C C X I I

In blesséd dreams and languishing delight,
I grasp a shade, and chase the summer breeze,
and swim alone through vast and depthless seas,
I build upon the sand, in wind I write.
　　I gaze upon the sun whose flaming light
has caused my strength of vision to decrease,
and mounted on a lame and weary beast
I hunt a wild relentless deer in flight.
　　Numb and blind to all except my pain,
I cry to Love, my lady and to Death,
who grant no solace for my wretched state.
　　Thus has this love of twenty years obtained
but tears and sighs and sorrow with each breath,
beneath such stars I took the hook and bait!

## C C X V

In nobil sangue vita umile e queta,
et in alto intelletto un puro core,
frutto senile in sul giovenil fiore,
e 'n aspetto pensoso anima lieta,

  raccolto ha 'n questa donna il suo pianeta,
anzi 'l re de le stelle, e 'l vero onore,
le degne lode, e 'l gran pregio, e 'l valore,
ch'è da stancar ogni divin poeta.

  Amor s'è in lei con Onestate aggiunto,
con Beltà naturale Abito adorno,
et un atto che parla con silenzio,

  e non so che nelli occhi, che 'n un punto
pò far chiara la notte, oscuro il giorno,
e 'l mel amaro, et adolcir l'assenzio.

# C C X V

In noble blood serene and humble ways,
in seasoned mind a heart as pure as spring,
wisdom's harvest in youthful blossoming,
a blissful spirit in a pensive gaze,
    were gathered all together by the grace
of heaven's stars, or rather heaven's king,
and joined in her, with every worthy thing,
that never poet had the skill to praise.
    She has within her love and purity,
a look that speaks with silence in her eyes,
and loveliness by gentle habit graced,
    and something in her glance that suddenly
can dim the day, or light the evening sky,
make honey bitter, and sweeten absinthe's taste.

# C C X X I V

S'una fede amorosa, un cor non finto,
un languir dolce, un desiar cortese,
s'oneste voglie in gentil foco accese,
un lungo error in cieco laberinto,

    se ne la fronte ogni penser depinto,
od in voci interrotte a pena intese,
or da paura, or da vergogna offese,
s'un pallor di viola e d'amor tinto,

    s'aver altrui più caro che se stesso,
se sospirare e lagrimar mai sempre,
pascendosi di duol, d'ira e d'affanno,

    s'arder da lunge et agghiacciar da presso,
son le cagion ch'amando i' mi distempre,
vostro, donna, 'l peccato, e mio fia 'l danno.

# C C X X I V

If a loving heart and honest praise,
a happy woe, a yearning without blame,
a pure desire born of noble flame,
an endless straying through a tangled maze,

if a brow with every thought ablaze,
or a whisper, hesitant and lame,
pausing now for fear and now for shame,
if a pallor tinted by love's rays,

if feeding on despair and wrath and fear,
if holding someone dearer than one's life,
and languishing alone without relief,

if burning from afar and trembling near,
are all occasions for my bitter strife,
yours, lady, is the guilt, and mine the grief.

# C C X X I X

Cantai, or piango, e non men di dolcezza
del pianger prendo che del canto presi;
ch'a la cagion, non a l'effetto intesi
son i miei sensi vaghi pur d'altezza.
    Indi e mansuetudine e durezza
et atti feri et umili e cortesi,
porto egualmente, né me gravan pesi,
né l'arme mie punta di sdegni spezza.
    Tengan dunque ver me l'usato stile
Amor, madonna, il mondo, e mia fortuna,
ch'i' non penso esser mai se non felice.
    Viva o mora o languisca, un più gentile
stato del mio non è sotto la luna,
sì dolce è del mio amaro la radice.

# C C X X I X

I sang, and now I weep, and find my pain
as pleasing as I found the songs before,
and of my woes no longer seek a cure,
for with the cause my senses would remain;
   nor of the cruel effects do I complain;
her scorn, her sweetness spark in me no war:
a smile, a frown, I equally endure,
nor is my armor shattered by disdain.
   Then let the world, my lady, and my fate
afflict me in their fashion, now and soon,
yet I shall count my happiness complete;
   for though I live or die, a finer state
than mine does not exist beneath the moon,
the root of all my sorrow is so sweet.

# C C X X X I V

O cameretta che già fosti un porto
a le gravi tempeste mie diurne,
fonte se' or di lagrime notturne,
che 'l dì celate per vergogna porto.

O letticciuol che requie eri e conforto
in tanti affanni, di che dogliose urne
ti bagna Amor con quelle mani eburne,
solo ver me crudeli a sì gran torto!

Né pur il mio secreto e 'l mio riposo
fuggo, ma più me stesso, e 'l mio pensero,
che seguendol talor levommi a volo;

e 'l vulgo, a me nemico et odïoso
(chi 'l pensò mai!), per mio refugio chero:
tal paura ho di ritrovarmi solo.

# C C X X X I V

Oh little room who used to be a port
of calm before the stormy day's return,
now every night with tears and sighs you burn
that all day long I silently support.
   Oh little bed who were a tranquil fort
in all my war, what deep and bitter urns
do Love and those fair hands now overturn
upon the silence of my calm resort!
   Nor is it from my solitude I flee,
but more so from myself and from my mind,
upon whose wings so often I have flown;
   and in the crowd, my bitter enemy,
a comfort and a refuge now I find:
so greatly do I fear to be alone.

*After the Death of*
*Lady Laura*

# C C L X I X

Rotta è l'alta colonna e 'l verde lauro
che facean ombra al mio stanco pensero;
perduto ho quel che ritrovar non spero
dal borrea a l'austro, o dal mar indo al mauro.
Tolto m'hai, Morte, il mio doppio tesauro
che mi fea viver lieto e gire altero;
e ristorar nol pò terra né impero,
né gemma orïental, né forza d'auro.
Ma se consentimento è di destino,
che posso io più, se no aver l'alma trista,
umidi gli occhi sempre, e 'l viso chino?
O nostra vita ch'è sì bella in vista,
com perde agevolmente in un matino
quel che 'n molti anni a gran pena s'acquista!

# CCLXIX

The lofty column and the laurel tree
which used to give me shelter in my war,
are lost, although I seek forevermore
from pole to pole, from east to western sea.
    Death, you have deprived me suddenly
of my double wealth and left me poor;
you've taken what no kingdom can restore
nor gold or orient pearl bring back to me.
    But if this be what destiny ordain,
what can I do but wander in despair,
my eyes cast down, and spirit full of pain?
    Ah that this life of ours, which seems so fair,
can lose so swiftly what it strove to gain
throughout so many years, and with such care!

## CCLXXXVIII

I' ho pien di sospir quest'aere tutto,
d'aspri colli mirando il dolce piano,
ove nacque colei ch'avendo in mano
meo cor in sul fiorire e 'n sul far frutto,

è gita al cielo, ed hammi a tal condutto,
col subito partir, che di lontano
gli occhi miei stanchi lei cercando invano,
presso di sé non lassan loco asciutto.

Non è sterpo né sasso in questi monti,
non ramo o fronda verde in queste piagge,
non fiore in queste valli o foglia d'erba,

stilla d'acqua non ven di queste fonti,
né fiere han questi boschi sì selvagge,
che non sappian quanto è mia pena acerba.

# C C L X X X V I I I

I've filled the air around with many a sigh,
gazing from these hills down to the plain
where she was born, who having held her reign
in my heart for many years gone by,

   has suddenly departed to the sky,
while alone and grieving I remain,
with weary eyes that search for her in vain,
so that no place they look upon is dry.

   There is no weed or stone within these hills,
nor tree or flower growing in these vales,
nor in these woods no blade of grass or leaf,

   nor in these fountains any drop that spills,
nor beast so wild that roams these mountain trails,
who does not know my deep and bitter grief.

# C C X C I I

Gli occhi di ch'io parlai sì caldamente,
e le braccia, e le mani, e i piedi, e 'l viso,
che m'avean sì da me stesso diviso,
e fatto singular da l'altra gente;

le crespe chiome d'or puro lucente
e 'l lampeggiar de l'angelico riso
che solean fare in terra un paradiso,
poca polvere son, che nulla sente.

Et io pur vivo, onde mi doglio e sdegno,
rimaso senza 'l lume ch'amai tanto,
in gran fortuna e 'n disarmato legno.

Or sia qui fine al mio amoroso canto:
secca è la vena de l'usato ingegno,
e la cetera mia rivolta in pianto.

## C C X C I I

The eyes of which my verses were so proud,
the arms and hands, the feet and form and face
that took my spirit from me by their grace,
and made me stand apart from all the crowd;
    the waving tresses like a golden cloud,
the gentle glow of that angelic gaze,
which made a heaven of an earthly place,
are now a bit of dust beneath a shroud.
    And yet I live, wherein I grieve and sigh,
left without the light I held so dear,
a battered boat caught in the tempest's eye.
    May all my songs of love be finished here:
the vein of my accustomed skill is dry,
and my sweet lyre turned to bitter tears.

# CCCII

Levommi il mio penser in parte ov'era
quella ch'io cerco, e non ritrovo in terra;
ivi fra lor che 'l terzo cerchio serra,
la rividi più bella e meno altera.

Per man mi prese e disse:—In questa spera
sarai ancor meco, se 'l desir non erra;
i' so' colei che ti diè tanta guerra,
e compié' mia giornata inanzi sera.

Mio ben non cape in intelletto umano:
te solo aspetto, e quel che tanto amasti
e là giuso è rimaso, il mio bel velo.—

Deh perché tacque? et allargò la mano?
ch'al suon de' detti sì pietosi e casti
poco mancò ch'io non rimasi in cielo.

# C C C I I

My spirit bore me upward toward the sphere
where she is now who dwelt on earth before,
and found her still more beautiful and pure,
and gentler and less proud than she was here.
   She took my hand and told me, "Never fear;
if hope fail not, you'll be with me once more;
I am the one who gave you so much war;
whose day was through before her night drew near.
   My bliss no mortal mind can understand;
I wait for you, and what you loved so much,
which lies below, my lovely mortal guise."
   Ah why did she cease to speak, and drop my hand?
There lacked but little at her words and touch
for me to have remained in paradise.

# C C C X I

Quel rosigniuol, che sì soave piagne,
forse suoi figli, o sua cara consorte,
di dolcezza empie il cielo e le campagne
con tante note sì pietose e scorte,
    e tutta notte par che m'accompagne,
e mi rammente la mia dura sorte;
ch'altri che me non ho di ch'i' mi lagne,
ché 'n dee non credev'io regnasse Morte.
    O che lieve è inganar chi s'assecura!
Que' duo bei lumi assai più che 'l sol chiari
chi pensò mai veder far terra oscura?
    Or cognosco io che mia fera ventura
vuol che vivendo e lagrimando impari
come nulla qua giù diletta e dura.

# *C C C X I*

That nightingale, who fills the evening sky
with mournful music by my window late,
perhaps bewails his fledglings or his mate
as he pours forth his sweet and lonely cry,
    accompanying my sorrow as I sigh
and recall my harsh and bitter fate,
for which I have my blindness to berate
since I thought a goddess could not die.
    How lightly duped is the unwary mind!
Those eyes that once outshone the sunlight's glow,
who would have thought that they could be dark earth?
    And now my cruel destiny, I find,
would have me learn through suffering and woe,
that nothing here below has lasting worth.

## CCCLVIII

Non pò far Morte il dolce viso amaro,
ma 'l dolce viso dolce pò far Morte.
Che bisgon' a morir ben altre scorte?
Quella mi scorge ond'ogni ben imparo;

e Quei che del suo sangue non fu avaro,
che col pè ruppe le tartaree porte,
col suo morir par che mi riconforte:
dunque vien, Morte, il tuo venir m'è caro;

e non tardar ch'egli è ben tempo omai;
e se non fusse, e' fu 'l tempo in quel punto
che madonna passò di questa vita.

D'allor innanzi un dì non vissi mai:
seco fui in via, e seco al fin son giunto,
e mia giornata ho co' suoi piè fornita.

# C C C L V I I I

Death cannot defile that lovely face,
but that sweet face makes bitter death seem sweet.
Is there another guide I need entreat?
for she escorts me to a better place;
   and He who shed his blood to give us grace,
and trampled hell's dark portal with His feet;
His dying makes my comfort seem complete;
and therefore Death, I beg you come apace;
   nor tarry, for the time is now I pray,
or if not now, then it was long before:
the moment that my lady's life was done.
   Since then I have not lived a single day:
for at her journey's end, mine was no more,
and when her course was finished, mine was run.

# *C C C L X V*

I' vo piangendo i miei passati tempi
i quai posi in amar cosa mortale,
senza levarmi a volo, abbiend'io l'ale
per dar forse di me non bassi esempi.

Tu che vedi i miei mali indegni et empi,
Re del cielo invisibile immortale,
soccorri a l'alma disviata e frale,
e 'l suo defetto di tua grazia adempi;

sì che s'io vissi in guerra et in tempesta,
mora in pace et in porto, e se la stanza
fu vana, almen sia la partita onesta.

A quel poco di viver che m'avanza
et al morir degni esser tua man presta:
tu sai ben che 'n altrui non ho speranza.

# *C C C L X V*

I go repenting of the years gone by
in which I chose to love a mortal thing,
so that my spirit has not taken wing,
having all the while the strength to fly.
　　You who see my sorrow from on high,
immortal Lord, unseen almighty king,
grant me solace for my wandering,
have mercy on each undeserving sigh;
　　that if I lived in tempest and in war,
I die in peace, and if my life was vain,
You grant at least the parting may be pure.
　　To aid my final days I pray You deign,
and at the end escort me to Your shore;
You know for me no other hope remains.

# *Notes*

I
Although it begins the *Rime sparse,* this poem was apparently written after the others, and serves as introduction and apology for the work.

II
In a sense, this is the first poem of the *Rime sparse,* as it describes Love's victory over the poet; that is, when he first fell in love with Laura.
1–2. The "thousand wrongs" are the many times the poet has resisted Love's attacks in the past.
12. *the steep and lofty hill:* reason

IX
1. *the planet that denotes the hour:* the sun
2. The sun is in Taurus from April to May.

XVI
10. *the likeness:* the Veronica, a cloth preserved in St. Peter's Basilica, on which the features of Christ were said to have been imprinted when he wiped his face with it.

XXI
12. The line is a bit ambiguous; he probably means that if his heart departed from nature's course, he would die.

XXXVI
7. Suicide is, of course, forbidden to him by religion.

XLIV
1–4. The lines describe Caesar, who wept to learn that his son-in-law, Pompey, had been slain by the Egyptian king Ptolemy.
5–8. This refers to David, who mourned, respectively, for Absalom and Saul. The mountain had good cause to complain: when

David found out that Saul had killed himself on it, he cursed it, making it infertile.

### LIV
5. *I heard a voice ring out from far away:* his conscience
10. *when it was barely noon:* before his life was half over

### LXII
This commemorates the calendar date of Christ's crucifixion (April 6), which is also the day on which Petrarch first saw Laura. Hence there is a double edge to the plea that he may remember the day's significance, for now, more than ever, Laura must be in his thoughts.
8. *the adversary:* the devil

### LXXV
8. *its guide:* i.e., the "gentle thought" of line 6

### XCIII
6. *lovelorn fold:* not literal for Petrarch's *amoroso coro* (chorus of lovers), but I think it captures some of the contemptuous irony in Love's tone.
9–12. Love is often depicted taking aim at his victim through the eyes of the beloved.

### CII
1–4. See XLIV. Here, Caesar's tears for Pompey are described as hypocritical.

### CXII
1. *Sennuccio:* Petrarch's friend, the poet Sennuccio del Bene, to whom several other of the *Rime sparse* are addressed.

### CXXXIII
13. In this poem I have attempted, perhaps audaciously, to duplicate one of Petrarch's numerous puns on his lady's name.

### CXC
One of Petrarch's most beautiful sonnets. The poet's chase of the unattainable white deer is exquisitely wrought, both poetically and symbolically. See Sir Thomas Wyatt's lovely rendition: "Whoso list to hunt."
9–11. The warning on the collar derives from a legend that tells how, three hundred years after Caesar's death, a deer was found wearing a collar with the inscription: "Noli me tangere, Caesaris sum." Caesar here is probably God.
12. See note to LIV, line 10.

106

### CCIX

1. *The hills:* Petrarch's beloved refuge of Vaucluse, near the city of Avignon where Laura lived.

### CCLXIX

1. *The lofty column and the laurel tree:* plays on the names of, respectively, Petrarch's dear friend, the cardinal Giovanni Colonna, and Laura, who both died of the plague in 1348. (In the *Rime sparse* Laura is frequently associated with the laurel.)

### CCLXXXVIII

2. *from these hills down to the plain:* from the hills of Vaucluse toward Avignon, where Laura lived.

### CCCLVIII

6. This is a reference to the legend of the harrowing of hell, in which Christ broke open hell's gate in order to lead the patriarchs to heaven.

# Index of First Lines in Italian

O cameretta che già fosti un porto  *86*
Or che 'l ciel e la terra e 'l vento tace  *66*
Or vedi, Amor, che giovenetta donna  *52*

Padre del ciel, dopo i perduti giorni  *38*
Passa la nave mia colma d'oblio  *72*
Perch'al viso d'Amor portava insegna  *36*
Perch'io t'abbia guardato di menzogna  *32*
Per fare una leggiadra sua vendetta  *12*
Più volte Amor m'avea già detto:—Scrivi  *44*
Ponmi ove 'l sole occide i fiori e l'erba  *58*

Quando 'l pianeta che distingue l'ore  *14*
Que' che 'n Tesaglia ebbe le man sì pronte  *30*
Quel rosigniuol, che sì soave piagne  *98*

Rotta è l'alta colonna e 'l verde lauro  *90*

Se la mia vita da l'aspro tormento  *16*
Sennuccio, i' vo' che sapi in qual manera  *50*
S'io credesse per morte essere scarco  *28*
Solo e pensoso i più deserti campi  *26*
Son animali al mondo de sì altera  *20*
S'una fede amorosa, un cor non finto  *82*

Una candida cerva sopra l'erba  *74*

Vergognando talor ch'ancor si taccia  *22*
Voi ch'ascoltate in rime sparse il suono  *10*

# Index of First Lines in English

The lofty column and the laurel tree *91*
Love and Fortune and my mind, made sore *55*
Love and I are vanquished by delight *63*
Love who see within this weary breast *65*
The lovely eyes that dealt unto my heart *41*

My spirit bore me upward toward the sphere *97*
My vessel with oblivion its freight *73*
My warrior, a thousand times have I *25*

Now Love, see how this lady, young and fair *53*
Now that earth and heaven and the breeze *67*

Oh little room who used to be a port *87*

The poor old man, arising grey and pale *19*
Put me where the sun burns cruel and bright *59*

Sennuccio, I would tell you how I fare *51*

That nightingale, who fills the evening sky *99*
There are some creatures with such flawless sight *21*
To take his sweet revenge on me at last *13*

Upon a river bank a pure white deer *75*

When the planet that denotes the hour *15*
When through the verdant meadows here and there *69*
With no more pleasure did her lover sigh *35*

You who hear within my scattered verse *11*